Accessible Landscapes

Designing for Inclusion

by

Philip S. Evans
Manager, Campus Grounds
Department of Plant Operations
San Francisco State University

and

Brian Donnelly
Assistant Professor
Department of Design and Industry
San Franscisco State University

Illustrated by

Robert Natata
Lecturer
Department of Design and Industry
San Francisco State University

A publication of **The ACCESSIBLE LANDSCAPES Project**
Originally funded in part by the National Endowment for the Arts
A Federal Agency
Design Arts Program - Universal Design
Under the name "Landscapes For All"

Published
by
The Department of Plant Operations
San Francisco State University
1600 Holloway Avenue
San Francisco, CA 94132
(415) 338-1568

Library of Congress Catalog Card Number 93-93726
ISBN 0-9641244-0-8

DEDICATION

To **Susan Goltsman**

Moore Iacofano Goltsman, Inc., Berkeley, California
whose revolutionary "Play for All" program provided the original inspiration
for the "Landscapes For All" grant.

Acknowledgments

We are indebted to the National Endowment for the Arts for a seed grant under their Design Arts Program. The support of NEA was essential for us to be able to embark on this project.

Special thanks are due to MIG, Inc. (Moore Iacofano Goltsman, Inc.), Berkeley, California, which introduced us to NEA, and helped us to properly focus and develop The ACCESSIBLE LANDSCAPES Project for the past two years. In their office, Sally McIntyre skillfully prepared our grant application, and Tim Gilbert provided insight thoughtfully and capably throughout the project. Through their ongoing professional work, and through their publishing division, MIG Communications, MIG, Inc. continues to improve the inclusiveness of urban landscapes throughout the world.

In addition, this work would not have been possible without the efforts of numerous individuals at San Francisco State University. In particular, we want to thank Anita Silvers, Professor of Philosophy, and tireless advocate of access issues and the role of gardens in enriching our lives. Her wise and timely counsel, administrative skill, and sensitive editing have been invaluable throughout the project. We also appreciate the considerable financial, material, and moral support of Robert Hutson, Director of Plant Operations, and Robert Quinn, Executive Director of Capital Planning and Programs. Molly Brodie, Director of Disabled Student Services, and the late Dr. Kirk MacGugan, Coordinator of Physical and Environmental Disability Programs, were very helpful and instrumental in providing guidance and focus groups for design review.

Ricardo Gomes, Assistant Professor and Director of the Design Center for Global Needs at San Francisco State University, deserves kudos for his innovative classroom explorations into new forms of accessible landscape furniture. His work helped generate a productive cycle of research into inclusive design throughout the department. We also thank Dr. James Bebee, Professor and Design Coordinator, and Dr. Wan-Lee Cheng, Professor and Chairman, in the Design and Industry Department for their support.

Thanks are due to Vicki Bohnhoff of Invisible Structures, Inc., Denver, CO, for her generous contribution of GrassRings Grass paving System for our research in improving turf access.

Finally, we owe a great debt to all those in our community who have taught us about living with disability, and offered their full and frank review of our efforts. We would like to express our special appreciation for the contributions of Alan Fisk, Susan Palmer, Alan Richardson, and Anna Perla Von Frederick, who first opened our eyes to the range and depth of access improvements needed in urban landscapes. Doreen Woods did extensive research into visual impairment. Barry Ryan, Barry Atwood, and Todd Groves also gave generously of their time and energy to help us understand accessibilty from a user's point of view.

Design Credits

The Authors and Illustrator

Some of the concepts presented in this book are a result of substantial creative work by the authors and illustrator. Some are our own modifications of existing products or ideas which have been suggested or partially developed and/or published by others. As it is impossible to assign individual credits accurately, we publish them all on an anonymous basis. It is our hope that those whose individual contributions will be recognized here will soon see the fruits of their labor manifested in new designs for public landscapes.

Accessibility Focus Groups

The following individuals participated in our focus groups. Their detailed examination of these concepts, and their candor in evaluating them from the standpoint of their experience with disabilities, provided a tremendous education to the authors. Many suggestions they made have been incorporated into these designs.

Mohammed Alkharji
Lawrence Jay Buchalter
Luis Calderon
Mikal Cartor
Melinda Cochran
Elizabeth Dunlap
Lavaun Heaster
Joyce Hill
Claudia Jung
Jane Kohner
Erica Li
Robert McCarthy
Mary Pat Radocy
Grayce Regan
Marisela Sanchez
Jennifer Walsh

Student Contributors

Students in the design classes of Professors Ricardo Gomes and Brian Donelly worked at length on a variety of projects exploring accessible landscape furniture and other features. We have not attempted to list all of these individuals by name, but the work was substantial and innovative.

Each of the following students has made a valuable contribution to the design concepts included in this book.

Pablo Bautista
Craig Clifford
Shawn Flanagan
David Herman
Jui-Yu Hsiu
Denise Onitsuka
Peter Maxwell
Lenny Page
Rick Park
Sarah Pearl
Mike Popso
Adam Rowe
Randy Sinksen
Chris Tibbets
Matt Waite
Jennifer Wong

A substantial portion of the descriptive text for the drawings was written by Diana Moissant. Her vivid writing embodies the joys of using our six senses in the landscape. Publication and cover design, typesetting, and publishing were accomplished with speed and agility by Duncan Sutherland.

About the Authors

Philip Evans is responsible for the development and maintenance of the grounds of San Francisco State University. He holds a B.S. degree in Soil Science and Plant Nutrition from the University of California, Berkeley, and a M.S. in Horticulture from the University of California, Davis, with additional postgraduate course work and research in Horticulture at Colorado State University. His professional activities include participation in the California Park and Recreation Society, Presidency of the Bay Area Landscape Supervisor's Forum, technical articles in trade and research journals, and vocational education.With over 25 years experience in landscape design and grounds maintenance, he is an advocate for the diverse and valuable contributions offered by our public landscapes.

Brian Donnelly received his Master's Degree from the Rhode Island School of Design in 1980. He is currently an Assistant Professor at San Francisco State University in the Department of Design and Industry, and the Director of Design and Manufacturing with the Design Center for Global Needs, located at SFSU. Prior to joining the faculty at SFSU he worked for four years as a Senior Designer with Interform, a product development firm located in Menlo Park, CA. He also operated his own design firm in Los Angeles, where he worked on a variety of products and exhibit designs. His teaching experience includes five years as lecturer in the Department of Design at UCLA, where he served concurrently as a research fellow with the UCLA Advanced Design Research Group, and two years as an Assistant Professor of Industrial Design at Southern Illinois University. Many of the designs in this report are the result of his creative efforts, and further development is ongoing in the Design Center for Global Needs.

Robert Natata teaches product illustration in the Department of Design and Industry at San Francisco State University. He received a Bachelor of Science Degree in Industrial Design from the California State University at Long Beach. Apart from illustration, graphic design, and promotional packaging and exhibit design, he has done extensive work in architectural and other three-dimensional modeling. He is currently concentrating on computer graphics, animation, and multimedia presentations.

Table of Contents

Introduction 10

Chapter 1
Disability 12

Chapter 2
Designing for Inclusion 13

Chapter 3
Inclusive Paths and Plazas 15

Orientation 15
Pavement Access Coding 16
Non-Visual Cues 18
Virtual Reality Maps 20
Talking Maps 22
Lightbars 24
Way Stations 26
Play Stations 28

Chapter 4
Inclusive Furniture 30

Halfseats 31
The Open Bench 32
The Pipe Bench 34
The Sliding Picnic Bench 36
Swinging Seats 38
Springing Seats 40
Multi-height Seating 42
Stacking Blocks 44
Transfer Points 46
Deep Seats 48
Seating Alcoves 50
An Amphitheater for All 52
The Flexible Fountain 54

Chapter 5
Creating a Planted Environment . 56

Bringing Nature to People
in an Urban Environment 56
Access to Turf 58
Wheel Support Systems for Turf,
Sand, and Loose Aggregate Paths 58

Afterword 59

The Next Step 59
Video Presentation 59
Contact Us 59

Selected References 60

Introduction

The ACCESSIBLE LANDSCAPES *Project*

Background to the Project

America's public landscapes have traditionally been designed based on criteria appropriate to only the non-disabled population. As regulations have begun to dictate the need for access, we have seen a proliferation of ramps, railings, and other improvements. Unfortunately, some of these new features in access have been obtrusive or otherwise dysfunctional in terms of the overall use and enjoyment of the site. Despite federal and state legislation, most persons with disabilities still have limited access to the pleasures of public landscapes.

The ACCESSIBLE LANDSCAPES Project was conceived in 1990 as a logical extension of the excellent work in park and playground access by the firm of Moore Iacofano Goltsman, Inc. Their program was published in 1987 under the title "Play For All" (MIG Communications, 1802 5th St, Berkeley, CA 94710).

We believe it is possible and practical to design more accessible landscapes, and that access improvements can meet the needs of a wide range of people. The ACCESSIBLE LANDSCAPES Project is dedicated to these principles.

People and Institutions Involved

Seed money was provided by the National Endowment for the Arts, under the Design Arts Program. Throughout the project we have had the expert assistance of Moore Iacofano Goltsman, Inc., Berkeley, California.

Administrative and design costs were borne by San Francisco State University, primarily through the Department of Plant Operations and the Department of Design and Industry. The Department of Disabled Student Services and the Campus Disability Coordinator provided guidance.

Our Process

We held a series of focus group sessions with those who have experience with disability, and scheduled design development sessions between, returning to the same or different groups with evolving concepts for new furniture and other features which address the need to make the urban landscaped environment more user-friendly for all of us.

Our Goals

To stimulate discussion and further innovation throughout the professional community.

To help create a new vocabulary of inclusion, and a new standard for design of accessible, inclusive landscapes.

To promote the development of user-friendly public landscapes throughout the world.

Chapter 1

Disability

A disability is legally defined as "a physical or mental impairment which substantially limits one or more major life activity." Approximately 43 million American men, women, and children experience some degree of disability. Whether this disability is congenital or acquired later in life, disability is a part of life for many of us.

Disabilities can range from a permanent condition, such as blindness, quadriplegia, or schizophrenia, to more temporary states such as a broken arm, whiplash injury, or the effects of prescription drugs. Heart disease, diabetes, and muscular incoordination, among other conditions, also limit a person's activities. Aging people may suffer from a multitude of disabling conditions including paralysis, Alzheimer's, arthritis, and cataracts.

In a broad sense, disability affects us all daily. We all experience temporary impairments of our own ability daily when we have blisters, bruises, or babies in our arms. At those times we learn a little bit more about the nature of disability.

It is not therefore a question of 'if' we become disabled, but rather 'when'. Very likely, every living person on the planet will be disabled either temporarily or permanently at some point in their life.

Disability should not mean exclusion: each and every one of us is a unique and valuable member of our society. We all should be able to go anywhere and to enjoy the full range of experience that our public landscapes have to offer.

Chapter 2

Designing for Inclusion

"**Inclusion**" implies welcome.
"**Access**" only implies open doors.

With the advent of the Americans with Disabilities Act, ramps and railings are proliferating. Where it was once standard practice to use steps, landscape architects now face daunting engineering challenges to use long ramps without breaking up the site into pieces which are too small to function as effective public spaces. With all the new regulations, some newly designed spaces may not seem very user-friendly.

These new requirements, however, offer an opportunity to redesign our environment based on the principle of inclusion. After all, we are designing for our neighbors, friends, relatives, and visitors, for our entire community, for people of every description wishing to enjoy our precious landscape. We can design the structures in every space to be more comfortable for those of us who are blind, deaf, mobility impaired, or otherwise disabled. We can design spaces to facilitate participation by anyone and everyone regardless of their physical condition or any accompanying mobility equipment. Let's offer choice and selection, in addition to access. Our new public spaces will then better serve our broad and multi-faceted society.

User-friendly Site Planning

Most people enjoy the natural world, even in the reduced and constrained form of many urban landscapes. Our pleasures range from physical recreation to spiritual rejuvenation. When the weather is good, there are few people who don't want to enjoy the beauty and sensory richness of the landscape. Urban landscape spaces hold great potential for recreation, conversation, reflection, observation, and meditation. We need to make sure these spaces work for all of us.

In the following pages, we have attempted to illustrate how landscapes can be developed which accommodate the variety of physical needs of people. We have also tried to facilitate a full range of sensory experience in the landscape: textures, smells, sounds, and views.

Confident mobility and sensory access are both highly important to enrichment of our urban experience. Even the most wonderful landscape will be essentially inaccessible to anyone preoccupied with just keeping their balance. The struggle to get a wheelchair out of a rut or the discomfort of crossing a heavily textured surface can be great enough to outweigh the potential benefits of an experience of natural beauty. Navigating through a public landscape can be also be a fearsome experience for someone with low vision. Pavement edges, where the landscape begins, are where safety ends for those who have lost their sight. Even for the sighted, being lost distracts terribly from the enjoyment of a landscape.

Unobstructed walkways with gentle slopes are a fundamental part of a welcoming landscape. Grips, guides, and places to rest are also needed throughout the landscape to offer assistance in getting around comfortably. These need to be available, yet unobtrusive. The choice of materials and forms should not single out any landscape feature as being for "the disabled."

The plants in the landscape which are closest to walkways and benches are most often planted below knee level. The wonders of the landscape are therefore just as distant from people who find it difficult or inconvenient to bend down as they are from those who cannot bend down. We can solve that by doing a better job of bringing the landscape to people. Raised planters are the most common and most effective answer. They may need to cantilevered so that we can comfortably approach them without bumping knees or wheels. We can also integrate plants into other landscape furniture in a variety of ways.

We need to redesign many of our site utilities, such as picnic tables and drinking fountains, which don't work for anybody very well. Simple, maintenance-free mechanisms are important. Modular construction is often desirable, where a few types of manufactured units may be arranged in a multiplicity of ways. Using recycled plastic and other new materials may reduce expense and provide new standards of durability. All these considerations also make improved site furniture more financially accessible!

Even that familiar stalwart of the landscape, the park bench, doesn't serve our whole community well. We heard a lot in our focus groups about the need for varied heights, better means of transfer from wheelchairs to benches, more comfortable seats and surfaces, and better backrests.

Chapter 3

Inclusive Paths and Plazas

Orientation

The first task for any visitor to a park, school, or other institution is to make sense of the site. Where is the main entry, the main pathway, the main office, or other center of activity? Where are the services?

Signs

Effective signage is an art. One must find the right balance between visual clutter and necessary information. Lettering styles and sizes need to be adjusted for the distance from which people need to read them. Considerable work is being done to develop universal graphic symbols to quickly communicate important information.

Other Visual Clues

A significant number of people cannot read comfortably, because of educational deficiencies, non-native languages, learning disabilities, or visual impairment. Some people are too busy to read. Other visual cues are needed.

For the sighted population, a bright and beautiful flower bed will attract attention. People will move towards it. Murals or inviting sculpture may offer an equivalent attraction. Any landscape feature that is attractive at a distance can be used to lead people to the central plaza, administrative office, or ticket booth. If the hierarchy of attractiveness corresponds with the priority of the location, the site makes sense. Things seem to work together. It is more comfortable.

Pavement Graphics

Many new paving technologies and products are emerging which allow free use of color and textural variation in paving. It is easy now to use a variety of familiar and subliminal codes in our design. Circles or radiating lines focus attention on their geometric center. Contrasting pavement colors or textures can serve as warning areas bordering benches and other stumbling hazards. They can also serve as frames or highlights to draw attention to desirable features. Continuous strips of color can lead visitors from one area of high interest to another, or, for example, from a bus stop to the information center. This convenience is often found in hospital hallways.

However, color blindness is common among men, and many people have visual impairments during their lives. Distinct contrasts between light and dark colors, rather than subtle color variations, are most easily observed by those with visual impairments. More research is needed to define the appropriate colors and dimensions needed for effective pavement graphics.

Pathway Access Legends

We propose the development of a simple access coding system for pathway circulation on busy sites. These symbols will readily identify for users any changes in the kind of walkway surface they will encounter, the slope, and any obstacles to wheeled mobility. The familiar blue and white wheelchair symbol offers insufficient information. In many situations, the distance and destination are also useful. With such codes the choice of path across a large site becomes easier for everyone.

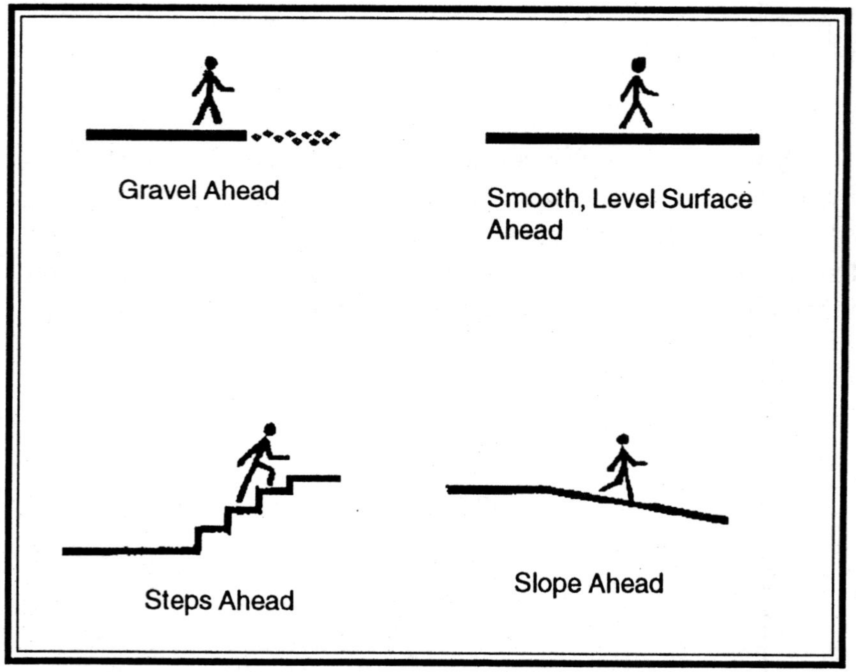

Sample Pathway Access Legends

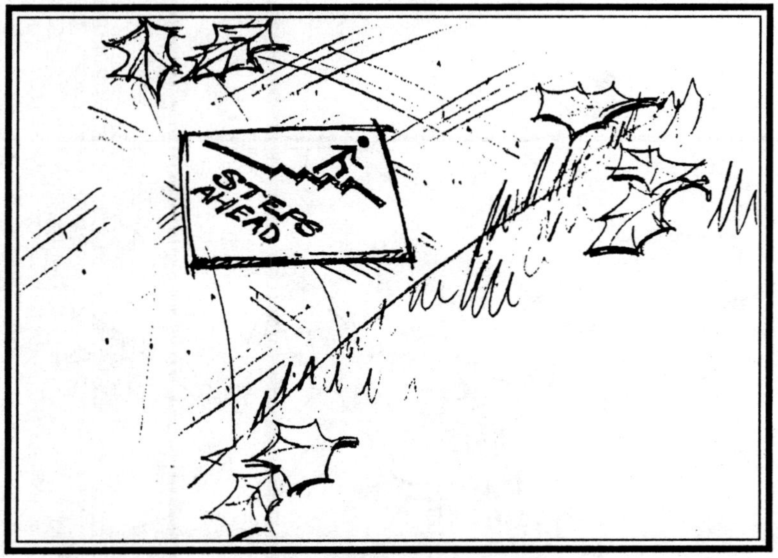

Pathway Access Legend in place on a walkway.

Pathway Access Legends assist visitors in selecting appropriate paths.

Non-Visual Cues

We may be able to remember, from our experience as children, how our sense of place was entwined with the sounds, smells, and textures of our environment. Such non-visual sensory elements create depth in our experience. These are also the cues which provide primary orientation to those who have temporary or permanent visual impairment.

A variety of non-visual sensory cues can be used to facilitate orientation. Associating different cues with specific parts of a site also helps to individualize these areas. This technique works with a wide variety of environments, from park settings to broad concrete plazas. Providing a multi-level sensory experience in our public areas is an important enhancement to the value of these capital-intensive investments. The more ways in which visitors can participate in the landscape the better!

Fragrances are also well-known for their impact on a visitor's experience of the landscape. Placing fragrant plants high enough and close enough to the walkways will provide a subtle and memorable enhancement. Sounds and fragrances help those with visual impairments orient themselves spatially.

Chimes and other wind-operated features generating pleasant sounds are highly useful in helping people orient to the environment. On the facing page you will see a conceptual fountain, designed with a sounding board beneath the falling stream of water. Alterations in the material of the sounding board allow designers to vary the quality and volume of the sound generated by the fountain.

Virtual Reality Maps

Virtual reality has become a reality!

It is now technically and economically feasible to design and produce a computer generated map which can render for the visitor an accurate visual experience of the site, as seen from eye-level, map view, or bird's eye perspective. The computer images can be designed to show in detail any feature on a particular pathway leading from the kiosk. For example, a visitor could request information on wheelchair accessible paths to a selected destination.

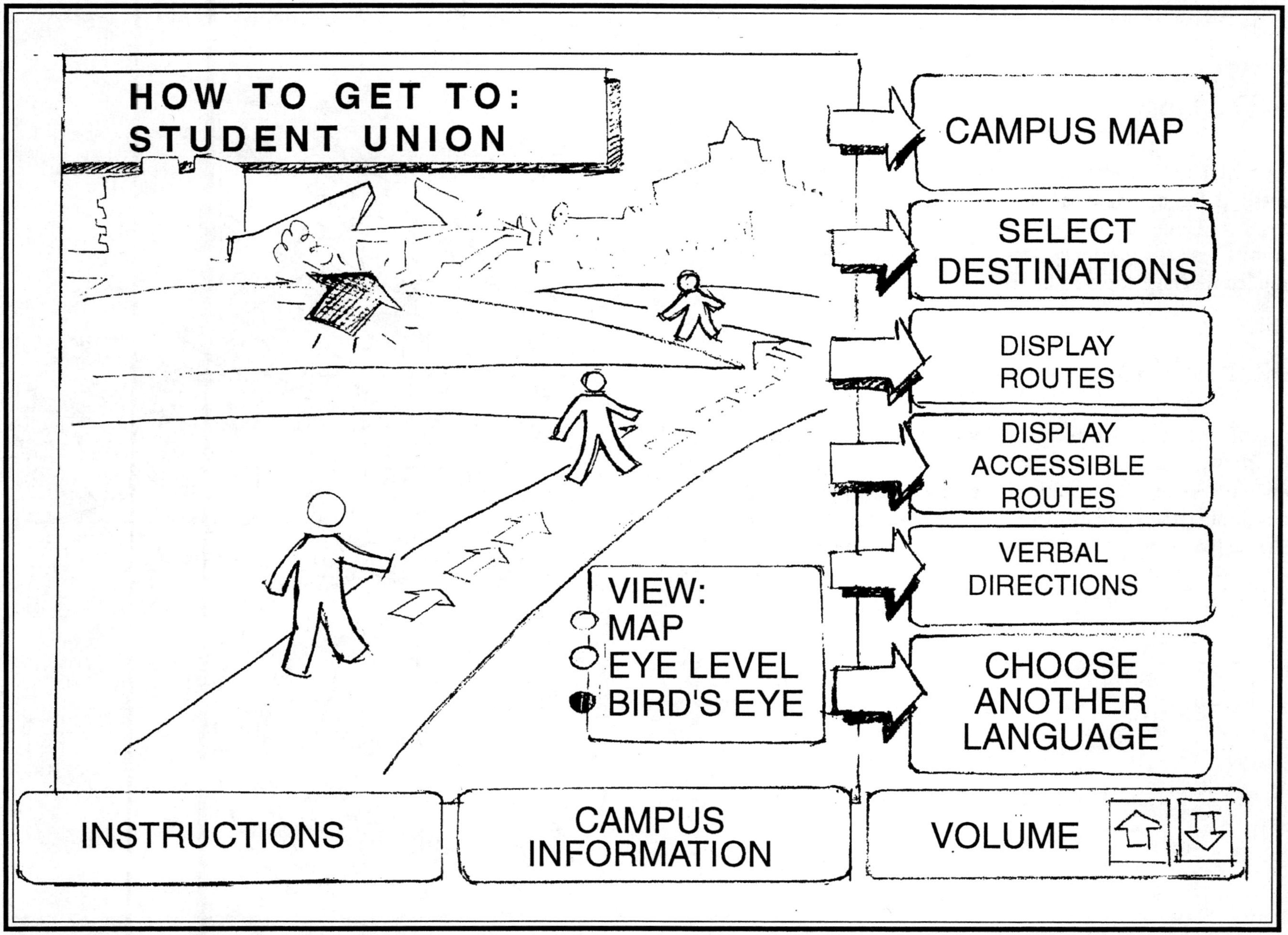
HOW TO GET TO:
STUDENT UNION
CAMPUS MAP
SELECT DESTINATIONS
DISPLAY ROUTES
DISPLAY ACCESSIBLE ROUTES
VERBAL DIRECTIONS
CHOOSE ANOTHER LANGUAGE
VIEW:
MAP
EYE LEVEL
BIRD'S EYE
INSTRUCTIONS
CAMPUS INFORMATION
VOLUME

3-D Maps

Maps of the site, mounted on pedestals or walls, are a prime method for communication of a wide variety of information to visitors. Three-dimensional maps add realism and facilitate orientation. These are becoming less expensive to make, using computer guided machine tools or lasers.

Tactile Maps

Tactile maps are intriguing for everyone, and particularly suited for those with impaired vision. Realistic visual representations are not always suitable for tactile maps, however. Special Guidelines for developing tactile maps are available from the American Printing House for the Blind (Please see Selected References on pg. 60).

Talking Maps

The most promising map technology for effective communication to a wide population is the "talking map". A large proportion of the visually impaired do not use Braille. Sighted visitors, too, generally prefer not to plow through extensive text and map keys. With a "talking map" at an entrance, all visitors can hear recorded information about different regions by touching parts of the map or legend. The quality and quantity of information which can be made available is extraordinary.

Talking Signs

"Talking Signs" technology consists of weatherproof infrared transmitters mounted over doorways, crosswalks, telephones, and other key locations. They are programmed to broadcast prerecorded information in a cone radiating from the transmitter. Individuals with special receivers are able to hear the transmissions. This technology is available now and is becoming popular due to its flexibility and relatively low cost.

A "Talking Map" mounted on a pedestal may be located at entrances or intersections.

Lightbars

In areas where adequate night lighting is not available, we propose the installation of lightbars along the edges of the primary circulation routes on the site. Lightbars are currently found in theatres and airplanes, as"Tivoli" or emergency egress lighting, and it is highly applicable to making the nighttime environment more comfortable for everyone where area lighting is inadequate.

Corresponding mini-lightbars bordering the pathways on pedestal maps could also be used to establish a clear correspondence between the map and the landscape.

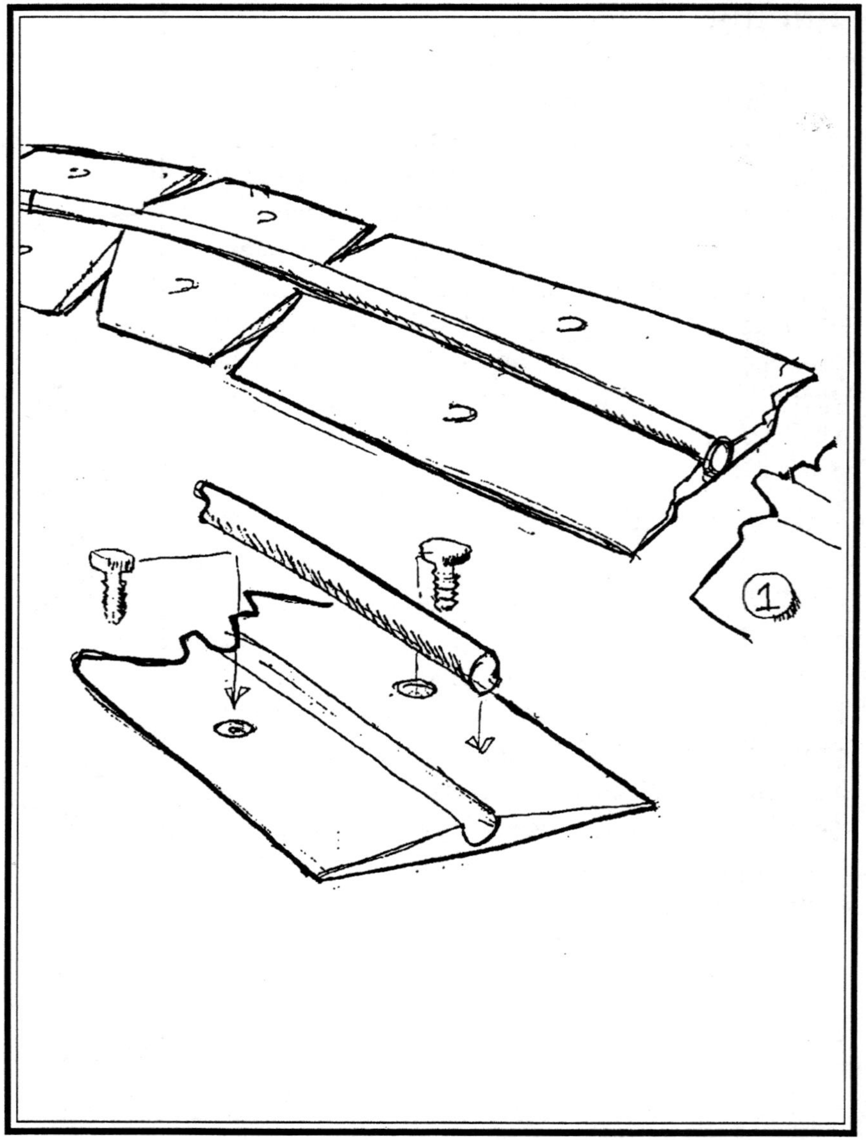

Tactile/High Contrast Edging

We show a fiberoptic pathway lightbar here as part of a tactile, high contrast, edging. The edge strip is designed for manufacture by extrusion. It may be affixed by screws or adhesives. Its low profile presents no tripping hazard. This strip has been designed to satisfy a number of needs. It defines the edges of paths clearly for the visually impaired, through either tactile reference with a cane or through the visual clue of a contrasting color. A similar strip laid across the path can indicate the presence of a pedestal map or other important site utility such as a telephone booth or drinking fountain.

As an enhancement, a variety of colors can be used to identify the hierarchy or direction of the path. For example, from a bus stop or other primary visitor entry point, directions to various features of the site could be as simple as following the color-coded edge strips.

Way Stations

What seems like a short walk to an able-bodied youngster may seem like quite a trek to many others. Many of us will experience difficulty at times negotiating long pathways, whether it is because we are recovering from surgery, having trouble breathing, or just have children and packages in our arms.

Way Stations provide a place to rest for a few minutes. Simple pedestals with rail grips and a place to set down a load may provide a welcome relief. Many features can be added, such as plantings, seats, maps, or lighting. The possibilities for design are exciting.

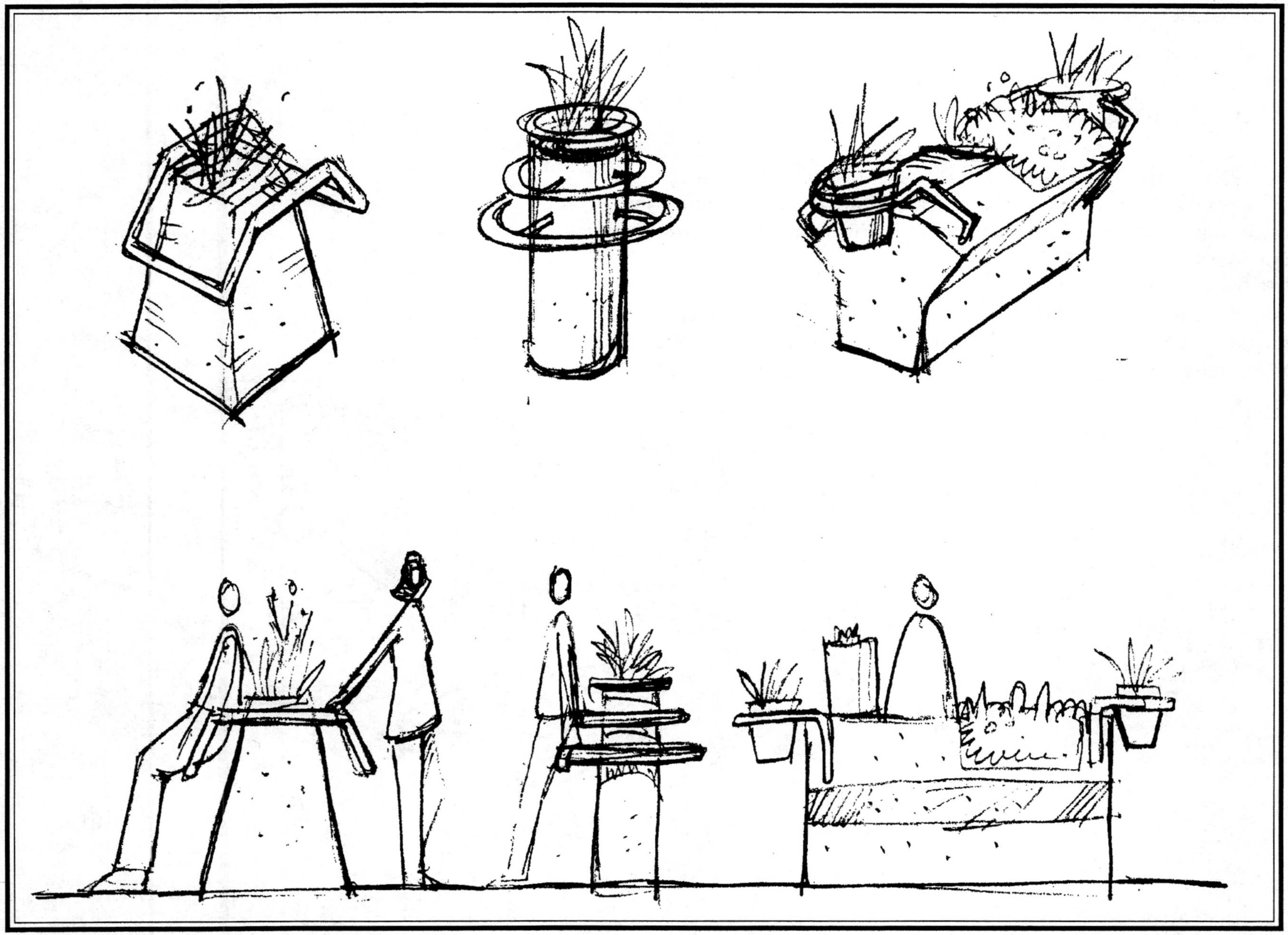

Play Stations

Play is not just for children. Lots of people like to play, and the delights of a playful interlude in the day can restore the spirit, allow for a constructive and gentle interaction between friends, and offer a stretch for our bodies.

We envision providing inclusive structures for play in public landscapes. Two examples are shown below and on the next page, a Sand and Water table, and a Jumble Gym, named for its myriad opportunities for physical activity.

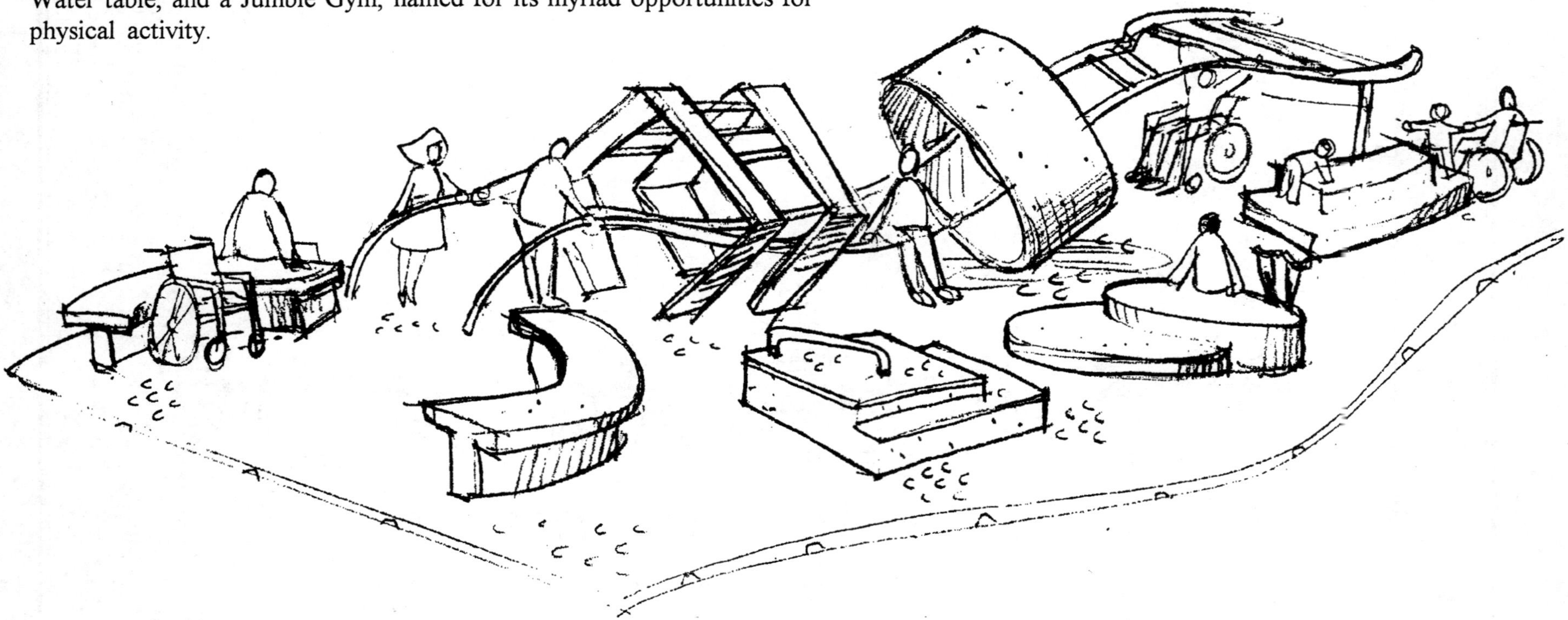

Chapter 4

Inclusive Furniture

Seating and Seating Arrangements

A Bench: an unchartered University of the mind, with courses shaped by curiosity and passion, and tuition only a willingness to speak and listen.

Can there be another public spot on earth so lavishly provisioned with people of so many shapes, colors, experiences, opinions, and ardencies?

What a clever scheme it is, to put benches here and there in public parks and places, inviting idle chatter. ...It is in this seminar of sovereigns ... that we may learn what our fellow citizens really think, often unveiling truths not otherwise available, and leading to an easy undoing of many of our certitudes.

Excerpted from
"Benches: The Thrones of our Republic" by P.M. Evans.
First published in the Christian Science Monitor, 1986.

Seats are one of the most important landscape elements. They serve as primary points of social contact and are used as temporary resting, eating, observation, and conversation spots.

Seats enable us to stop and experience our environment. On a windy day, we can watch the wind bend trees, ripple the surface of a pond, or waft clouds across the sky. We listen as the wind stirs bushes and rustles leaves. Seats can be tranquil places to sit, ponder, and watch the world lazily float by.

New Benches

We have focused our work primarily on sliding, swinging, and variable height seating. We have also explored other methods of expanding the usefulness of seating by changing the dimensions of seats, adding handles and other enhancements.

Inclusive seating is the single most critical factor in creating an accessible landscape. We hope to stimulate a renaissance in the art of seat-making.

Half Seats

Some of us may avoid sitting down if it is too difficult to get up again. The Half Seat is designed to offer a solution. Enough support is provided to bear one's weight and allow some relief, yet it is a simple matter to rise again to a standing position.

The Open Bench

You've experienced it: you're walking along searching for a place to sit. At last you find a bench, but there is one person sitting directly in the middle of it, arms stretched out and belongings scattered all along the bench. In this and many other situations, the unwritten laws of personal space create tension among people competing for sitting space on traditional benches.

Another limitation of the traditional bench is that the continuous seat surface makes it awkward to include a wheelchair user in a social group. Crutches, umbrellas, or strollers have to be placed somewhere, and often interfere with passing foot traffic. People in wheelchairs must either park at one end of the bench, or in the pathway in front of the bench, as illustrated below.

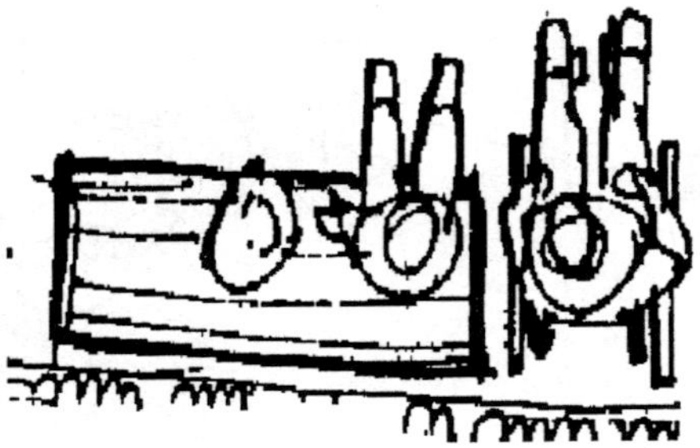

The Open Bench was designed to resolve these problems. Although this bench is shaped like a standard bench, it has one unusual, yet simple feature: seats that slide horizontally in both directions.

This sliding feature is possible due to a track built into the back of the bench. As the diagram on the opposite page shows, when seats are moved in either direction, an open space is created. The spaces can be adjusted to establish a comfortable space to one's neighbor, to accommodate bulky coats or packages, to accommodate a standing person or a wheelchair, a stroller, child's wagon, etc.

The seats are held in place by a friction brake, activated whenever the seat is pushed downward slightly. The seats are provided with spacing stops to prevent pinching when closing. Easily operable handles/armrests are designed for easy transfer and comfortable sitting.

The Open Bench can be manufactured in straight or curved sections of varying length, making it possible to use long bench sections in a variety of situations. This bench is safe, practical, low-cost, easy to maintain and combines the best in design and comfort: a truly versatile, inclusive, and accessible outdoor bench.

The Pipe Bench

Using this simple configuration of a curving pipe rail support, custom seating can be tailored to a site. Curved amphitheater style arrangements, sinuous tracks designed to integrate with the shapes of planting beds or winding paths, and a multitude of other effects are possible. The seats are provided with backs for comfort, and friction brakes to hold position when seated.

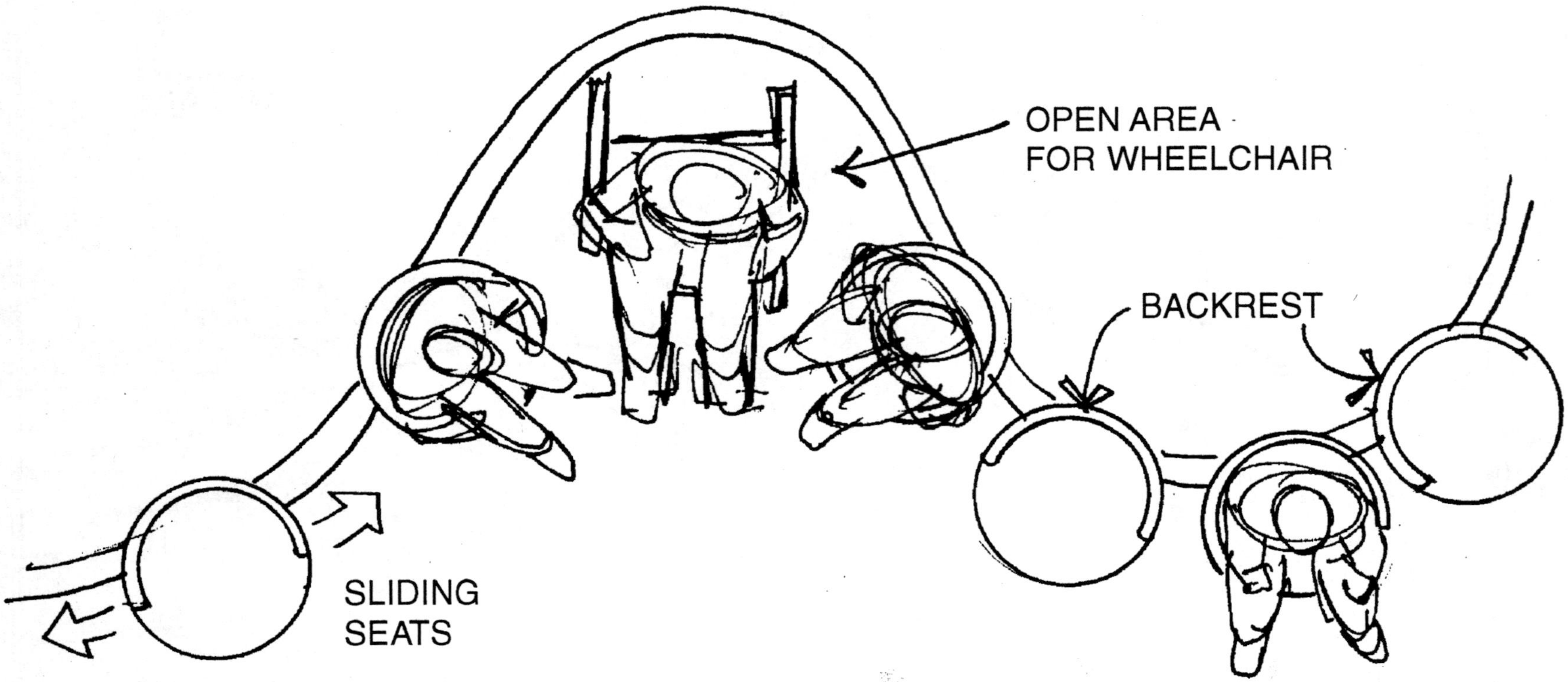

The Sliding Picnic Bench

In this bench a sliding seat again offers variable spacing. Each small bench is equipped with rollers, enabling them to slide back and forth. A friction brake controls the slide and assures safe seating.

Introducing spaces in the traditional continuous picnic bench allows creative and comfortable social arrangements. Children can be seated in the middle, yet escape to play when they are done with less disturbance to others. Wheelchair users have far more places available at the table. Coolers or picnic baskets can also be placed in the spaces for easy access.

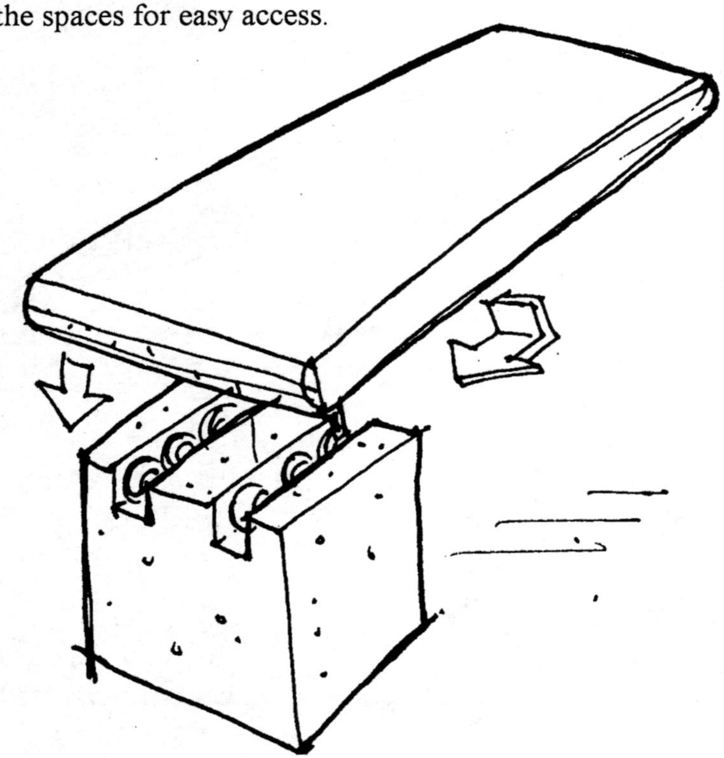

Swinging Seats

These seats are fixed on a hinge to eliminate loss from theft, yet can be moved as needed to accommodate the needs of those at the table.

Individual seats are mounted on a spiral screw posts, which can be screwed up or down to adjust the seat to a comfortable height. Backrests are provided for comfortable support.

Springing Seat

For many people, particularly the elderly, the decision to sit down can be difficult because of the stress and strain of getting down into and then back out of a standard seat. The following concept offers an alternative by which the spring loaded circular arms assist people when they start to recline and offers them a boost when getting up.

The raised flexible protrusions on the seat surface (please see inset detail) may be constructed of a variety of materials and in various dimensions. They may provide a cushioned surface, massaging action, or thermal insulation.

SIDE VIEW
SEAT
BACK
DETAIL

Multi-height Seating

Fixed wall seating is notoriously monotonous and has limited flexibility. The height of the wall is often determined by engineering requirements, such as the height of the earth to be retained behind it, or by reference to standard tables of seat height and construction costs.

Multi-height seating should be incorporated as often as possible into the landscape. Offering options in height makes the environment friendlier and more useful for everyone.

Some of the elderly and others who may have difficulty getting up from a full sitting position will prefer to sit on higher seats, reducing the lift needed to get back up. People using wheelchairs who wish to transfer to a bench often need to find a seat at the same height as their chair seat, for a comfortable transfer. Children also appreciate variable heights.

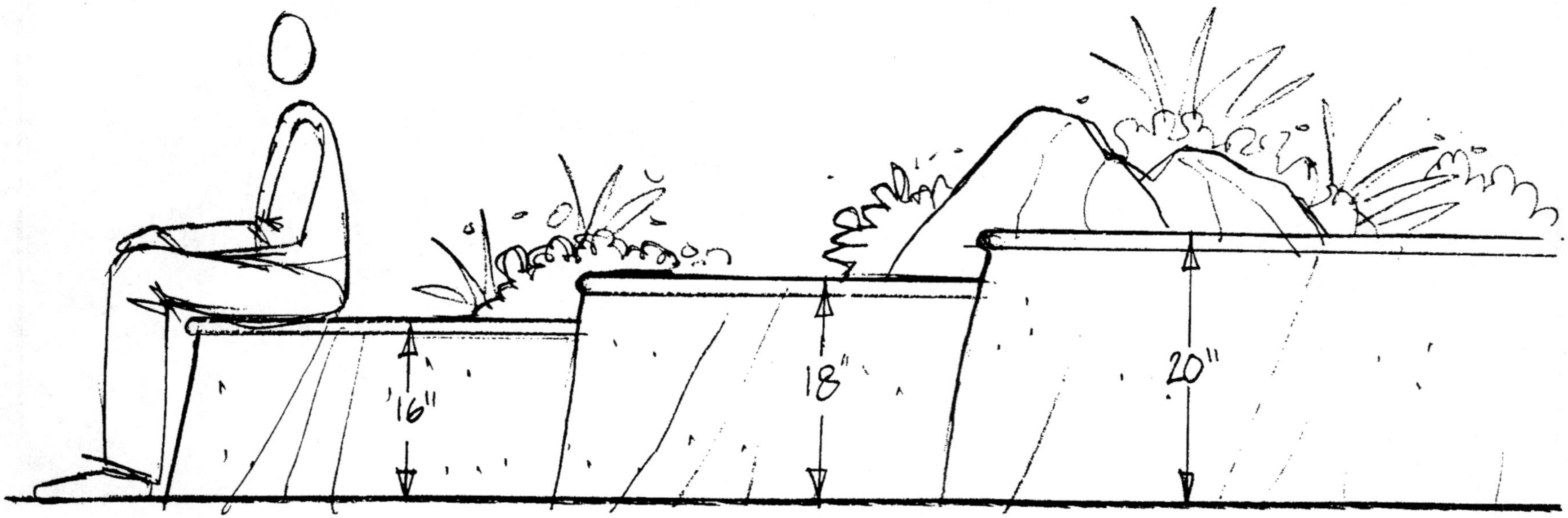

Stacking Blocks

Modular stacking blocks are a flexible and convenient seating arrangement. They are inexpensive to manufacture and install, and a wide variety of materials may be used in their construction. Here is an opportunity to develop a functional product of recycled plastic.

The goal is to provide gradually elevated and lowered heights for easy climbing and a variety of dimensions for comfort. The blocks may be assembled in any number of arrangements, joined in each corner. When necessary, blocks can be separated, re-attached, and stacked in new formations. To prevent loss and add stability, blocks may be solid, or filled with sand to weigh them down. As an added safety feature, all the edges on these boxes are rounded so there are no sharp corners. Fasteners may be hidden or recessed.

Transfer Points

Opportunities are traditionally limited for wheelchair users to transfer to a seat having more access to the landscape.

Some simple modifications to any seat wall will significantly increase access to the landscape beyond.

1. Offer multiple heights
2. Use a smooth hard plastic for a transfer surface to avoid abrading clothing when scooting
3. Use sloping rails as shown to accommodate various reaches and positions during transferring
4. Provide a backrest where possible

This is an artist's conception of variable height seating elements which transform the landscape into a more inviting and accessible setting. Note the grassy slope rising to meet the bench top in the foreground. A backrest is also provided, with grip rails inset in its surface.

Deep Seats

This is a multipurpose seat wall configuration to allow space for a variety of activities. One can spread out a lunch or board game, lay down to read, sit crosslegged, or transfer with legs outstretched.

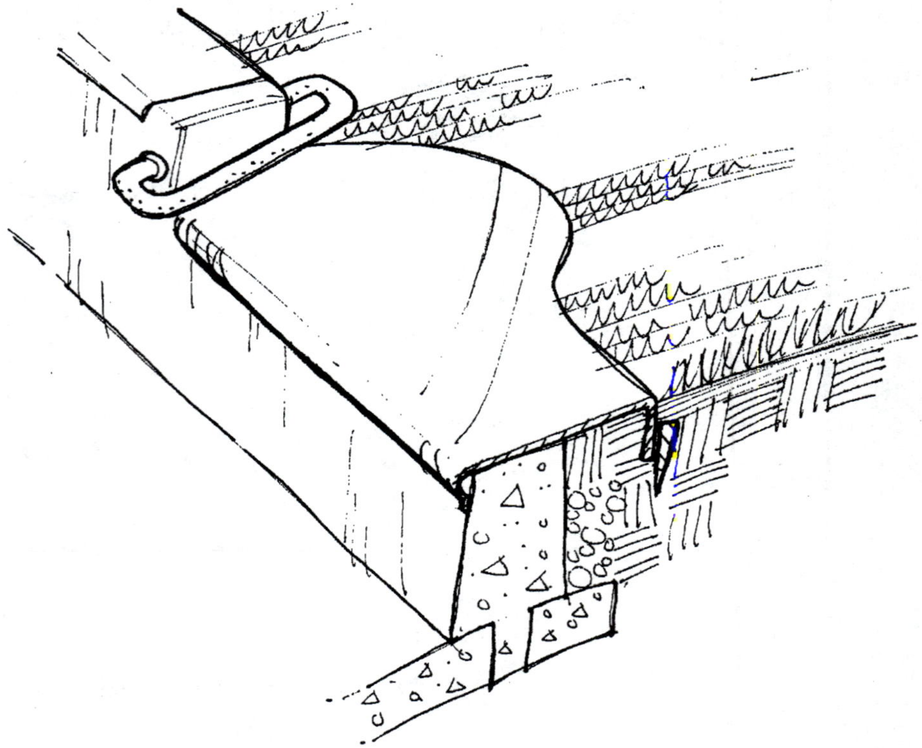

ANGLED
GRAB BAR

Seating Alcoves

The seating alcoves envisioned here are an enhanced version of the Deep Seats. Alcoves in the landscape provide a place to escape from foot traffic and everyday hustle and bustle. Alcoves are built right into the earth, so that the visitor is literally ensconced within the landscape. Designers have the option of using these alcoves instead of stepped retaining walls to convert sloping areas to comfortable seating.

These alcoves are conceived as modular units, manufactured from durable plastics. They are easily manufactured and shipped. The alcove seating surfaces are designed for smooth transfer from wheelchair to seat, and for easy scooting. They are deep enough to accommodate the same range of activities as the Deep Seat, but provide a more formal setting with a continuous backrest for comfort. The alcoves are equipped with handgrips, located at both ends.

Many backrest configurations are possible. The essential feature is a comfortable, contoured surface. Grips or movement assists can be built in to the backrest. The backrest can also incorporate natural objects such as boulders or finished log surfaces, to enhance the feeling of closeness with nature. Alcove seats are easy to clean, non-absorbent, and slightly pitched for efficient drainage.

Alcoves can be built into just about any landscape setting-- into small hills, along level walkways, or in sunken areas. Alcoves can also be placed just about anywhere: under trees, near fountains, and into buildings. They are shown here as semicircles, but many shapes will offer accessible seating. This is a concept which can be elaborated or simplified to suit any site.

An Amphitheater for All

The Amphitheater for All is designed with comfortable seating for everyone in mind. We've taken the timeless Greek amphitheater design and added enhancements so that universal access is achieved. Rather than having the disabled designated to a special seating section, our arrangement allows wheelchair users or others with mobility aids full freedom in choice of a seat. This design brings amphitheater seating into full conformity with new disability laws.

In the Amphitheater for All, seat rows and wide alleys alternate. Flip-up seats allow space for wheelchairs, strollers, etc. to be backed in against the back frame. This allows shoulder to shoulder seating and unobstructed foot traffic along the alleys.

The alleys are wide enough so that wheelchair users or people with canes will be able to move freely between rows of seats, even when the seats are occupied and flipped down. Ramped walkways provide access between rows. Where economic constraints dictate a denser packing of spectators, wide alleys can be provided less frequently, and still achieve a good distribution of inclusive seating. This amphitheater is designed for the comfort of all.

The Flexible Fountain

Drinking fountains are often at an uncomfortable or unreachable height, even the familiar “accessible” fountains. Sometimes, too, fountains are hard to use because the operating mechanism requires excessive hand or finger strength.

The Flexible Fountain offers adjustable height and position, and hands-free operation. The extending basin pivots easily in any direction. On the ground, directly beneath the basin, is a pressure plate. Standing or rolling onto the plate activates the water, for hands-free operation. As an added feature, the fountain’s basin is wide enough for hand-rinsing. An easily maintainable, clog-resistant drain is provided, too, since outdoor drinking fountains take a lot of abuse.

Accessibility for all is the goal of this design. Wheelchair users can easily use the fountain from a seated position and can operate the water valve by rolling onto the pressure switch. Children can also use this fountain without the help of adults. Everyone can drink without stooping or standing on toes!

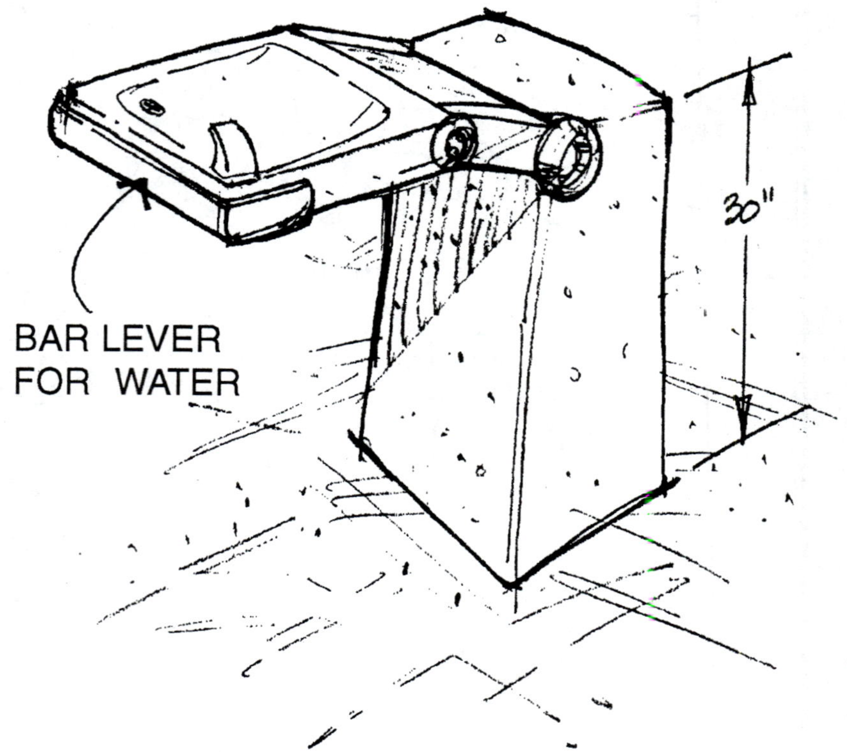

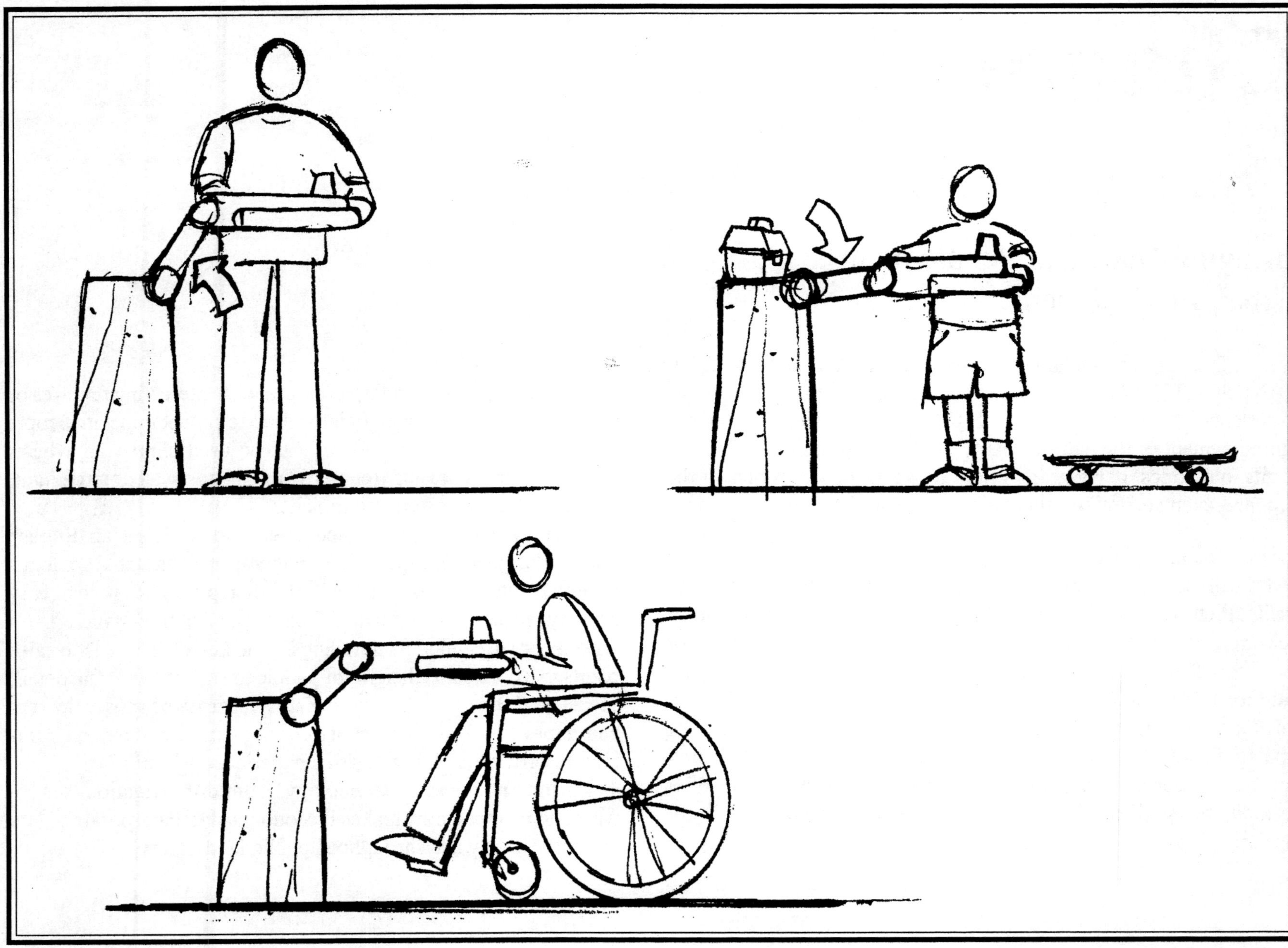

Chapter 5

Creating a Planted Environment

Bringing Nature to People in an Urban Environment

One of the fundamental missions of The ACCESSIBLE LANDSCAPES Project is to enable all people to more comfortably experience and appreciate nature. Sight, touch, and smell all enhance our enjoyment of the natural beauty of plants and flowers. Delicate plants, birdsongs, dewy grass, bright flowers, the warm rays of the sun, and even stormy weather offer primeval pleasures.

Imagine walking along a pathway and reaching up to touch and smell perfumed flowers that are hanging from an overhead trellis. Picture yourself sitting down at a table and being able to delicately caress the petals of poppies that are growing right out of the table. Think of what a nice change it would be to surround an outdoor telephone booth with raised planters so that a caller can smell a potpourri of fragrances, or look out to see a multitude of smiling flowers. Running one's fingers over a leaf and feeling unexpected sensations; inhaling the sweet, fragrant aroma of a daffodil; being dazzled by the vivid color contrasts of a floral display; this is all a part of becoming more intimate with nature.

Flowering vines and other plants with interesting textures or foliage colors can be brought into intimate connection with people in a variety of settings. Plants can be used almost anywhere: hanging from arches and trellises, climbing up a wall or streetlight, next to benches, in surprising niches.

"Bliss Boxes," nicknamed after Jeanne Bliss, an English garden designer who specializes in therapeutic gardens, are luxuriantly planted boxes intended to bring plants to within easy sensory access. Such planted boxes can be free-standing, on wheels, or suspended from railings. The key objective is to raise plants to a convenient height for people to enjoy their visual detail, scents, and textures. Aromatic plants, intricate or showy flowers and interesting leaf textures or other botanical features all combine to provide a highly positive experience of nature.

Modern landscape technology, from drip irrigation to self-watering planters, now makes it economical to incorporate plants in imaginative ways throughout public landscapes.

PLANTS

Access to Turf

It may be hard to believe at first that turf is not accessible by today's definitions. Wide open expanses of grass or small bermed lawns seem at first to be available and easy to use.

However, imagine for a moment the difficulties in riding a bicycle or walking with crutches on turf. The friction of grass blades is significant. It is enough to make mobility quite difficult for those using crutches, wheeled mobility aids, or simply unable to lift their feet. Turf is soft when wet, and this also aggravates mobility problems for everyone. No one enjoys sinking into wet grass.

Wheel Support Systems for Turf, Sand, and Loose Aggregate Pathways

Several manufacturers supply products intended to provide an subsurface structural support for occasional vehicle traffic on turf. One style is visible, made of concrete grids, in which the weight of the wheels is borne by the concrete, and grass or other ground cover may be planted in the spaces in the grids. Some supports are meant to be buried in the soil, sand, or other loose path material, and are constructed of various plastics to save weight and simplify installation.

On the other hand, these products do not offer a completely satisfactory solution yet. Due to their open grid construction, the earth in the spaces may be lower or higher than the edges. A wheelchair wheel faithfully transmits to the rider the profile of the ground in its path. Consequently, the hard edges of these support materials may create a more uncomfortable ride than the grass would ordinarily offer. In addition, if the turf wears away in an area, the structures will be exposed at the surface and catch on crutches or shoe heels. Those products with hard, uneven, or sharp edges can provide a hazard to people falling or kneeling on the grass. Those using canes or walkers will still find traversing grass difficult.

Products with a smooth surface support, soft plastic construction, and small cell diameter significantly improve the accessibility of turf, sand, crushed rock, decomposed granite and other variable surface materials by providing a solid subsurface base. One can't get stuck in a rut. The improvement in support and the ease of rolling a wheelchair is noticeable.

Afterword

The Next Step

We hope that our readers will join us in taking the next step - bringing these concepts to life. Opportunities for improved inclusion and access abound on every business and hospital campus, at every school and park, and every airport and transit station.

The new concepts presented here are schematic, and are meant to stimulate further innovation in design of landscape furniture and other features. The Design Center for Global Needs, here at San Francisco State University, is developing these and other concepts into working prototypes. We plan to install these new landscape features as they are developed in the living laboratory of our diverse, busy campus. The results of this research will be made available to the public in future publications.

Video Presentation

A video presentation is available summarizing our project and showing many of these products in lifelike animation and in actual landscaped settings. This is an extraordinarily effective tool for visualizing realistically the intrinsic value and impact of these innovations.

Contact Us

Professional collaboration is welcome as we carry out this exciting work. Individuals and organizations interested in supporting or participating in this effort should contact us in writing or via email.

Philip Evans (415) 338-1568.
Department of Plant Operations
email: pevans@sfsu.edu
or
Brian Donnelly
The Design Center for Global Needs
Department of Design and Industry
email: ricgomes@sfsu.edu
at
San Francisco State University
San Francisco, CA 94132

Selected References

Government Publications

The American with Disabilities Act: Title II Technical Assistance Manual. Washington, DC: U.S. Department of Justice - Civil Rights Division.

The American with Disabilities Act: Title III Technical Assistance Manual. Washington, DC: U.S. Department of Justice - Civil Rights Division.

California State Accessibility Standards - Interpretive Manual, 3rd. ed., July 19, 1989, Sacramento, CA: Office of the State Architect.

Design Guide for Accessible Outdoor Recreation - Interim Draft for Review, September, 1990. Washington, DC: U.S. Department of Agriculture, U.S. Department of Interior.

Federal Register, July 26, 1991. Part III: Nondiscrimination on the Basis of Disability by Public Accommodations and in Commercial Facilities: Final Rule. Washington, DC: Department of Justice, Office of the Attorney General.

Federal Register, July 26, 1991. Part IV: Nondiscrimination on the Basis of Disability in State and Local Government Services: Final Rule. Washington, DC: Department of Justice, Office of the Attorney General.

Federal Register, September 6, 1991. Part IV: Transportation for Individuals with Disabilities: Final Rule. Washington, DC: Department of Transportation.

Title 24, CCR: California Building Code, March 5, 1993. California State Accessibility Standards, Final Draft. Sacramento, CA: Access Compliance Section - Office of the State Architect.

Uniform Federal Accessibility Standards, February 1, 1992. Washington, DC: General Services Administration, Department of Defense, Department of Housing and Urban Development, U.S. Postal Service.

Other Publications

Adaptive Environments Center/Welch & Epp Associates (1986). *Access Improvements Workbook.* Boston, MA: Commonwealth of Massachusetts Division of Capital Planning and Operation, Executive Office for Administration and Finance, and Office of Handicapped Affairs.

Adaptive Environments Center/Welch & Epp Associates (1988). *Design for Access: A Guidebook for Designing Barrier Free State and County Building.* Boston, MA: Commonwealth of Massachusetts Division of Capital Planning and Operation, Executive Office for Administration and Finance, and Office of Handicapped Affairs.

American Printing House for the Blind, Inc. (1993). *Guidelines for the Design of Tactile Graphics.* Louisville, KY.

Barrier Free Environments, Inc. / Harold Russell Associates, Inc. (1980). *The Planner's Guide to Barrier Free Meetings.* Raleigh, NC: Barrier Free Environments, Inc.

Barrier Free Environments, Inc. (1991). *UFAS Retrofit Manual.* Washington, DC: Architectural and Transportation Barriers Compliance Board.

Barrier Free Environments, Inc. (1985). *The Arts and 504: A 504 Handbook.* Washington, DC: National Endowment for the Arts.

Bliss, Jeanne (1990) *Blueprint for a Hospital Courtyard Garden.* 37 Meadow Prospect, Wolvercote, Oxford, OX2 8PP England.

Center for Accessible Housing (1992). *The Fair Housing Accessibility Guidelines - Requirement #1: Analyzing Site Impracticality on Difficult Sites.* Raleigh, NC: Center for Accessible Housing.

Center for Accessible Housing (1992). *Recommended Supplements, Pertaining to Children's Environments, to the Uniform Federal Accessibility Standards.* Raleigh, NC: Center for Accessible Housing.

Duncan, John, et al. (1977). *Environmental Modifications for the Visually Impaired: A Handbook.* New York, NY: American Foundation for the Blind.

Enders, A. (1990). *Assistive Technology Sourcebook.* Washington, DC: RESNA.

Goltsman, Susan M., Gilbert, Timothy A., and Wohlford, Steven D. (1992). *The Accessibility Checklist: An Evaluation System for Buildings and Outdoor Settings.* Berkeley, CA: MIG Communications.

Lifchez, Raymond and Winslow, Barbara (1979). *Design for Independent Living.* Berkeley, CA: University of California Press.

Living Wall Garden Co. (1992) *Living Wall Garden Growing System* 2044 Chili Ave. Rochester, NY 14624.

Mace, Ronald L., Hardie, Graema J., and Place, Jaine P. (1991). *Accessible Environments: Toward Universal Design.* Raleigh, NC: Center for Accessible Housing.

Moore, Robin C., Goltsman, Susan M,. and Iacofano, Daniel S., editors (1992). *The Play For All Guidelines: Planning, Design and Management of Outdoor Play Setting for All Children, 2nd ed.* Berkeley, CA: MIG Communications.

Mueller, James (1990). *The Workplace Workbook.* Washington, DC: RESNA

Nordhaus, R.S., Kantrowitz, M. & Siembieda, W.J.(1984). *Accessible Fishing: A Planning Handbook.* Santa Fe, NM: New Mexico Natural Resources Department.

Ostroff, E. (1978). *Humanizing Environments*. Cambridge, MA:The Word Guild.

Peoples Housing, Inc. (1983). *Retrofitting Public Restrooms for Accessibility*. Sacramento, CA: California Department of Rehabilitation.

Peters, G.A. (1986). Warning Signs and Safety Instructions: Covering All Bases. *Security and Fire News.* Jan/Feb. 1986.

Robinette, G. (1985). *Barrier-Free Site Design: Anyone Can Go Anywhere.* New York: Van Nostrand Reinhold.

Ruddy, N. (1981). ANSI A117.1 (1980) Survey Checklist. *Access Information Bulletin.* Washington, DC: NCBFE.

Rutledge, A. & Molnar, D.J. (1986, 2nd.ed.). *Anatomy of a Park: The Essential of Recreation Area Planning and Design.* New York: McGraw Hill.

Talking Signs, Inc. *The Accessible Planet.* 812 North Blvd. Baton Rouge, LA. 70802

Zirpolo, N. (19876). Plan Checking Report, Flood Park Barrie Free Accss Design Project, San Mateo County Parks and Recreation Division, Department of Environmental Management, San Mateo, CA.